Embracing Your Identity and Living Your Purpose

Dr. Daren Waters, Sr.

Embracing Your Identity and Living Your Purpose

by

Dr. Daren Waters, Sr.

First Edition 2015

Copyright © 2015 by Dr. Daren Waters, Sr.

ISBN # 978-0692418314

Cover Design by: AnnVelyn Carter

Edited by: Bonita Jewell and Peggie Pearl

Published by: Valdosta Coaching Network

Printed in USA by Create Space

Dedication

To my God, my family, my friends and all who have added value to my life to live my God-given purpose.

Table of Contents

Acknowledgements

I give thanks to the King of kings for the grace, inspiration, and passion to communicate to and with others the significance of our uniqueness and the need to live our purpose in life.

I want to thank my lovely bride, Carolyn, and our children – Daren, Jr., Daroslyn, and Dariana – for your continuous love, prayers, and support of the fulfillment of writing our first book. I love you all so much!

Special thanks to Cornelius, Kristy, Corey, and Kara Clark for your reviews and feedback. I express gratitude to Patricia Bryant and Peggie Pearl who, without reservation, partnered with me to provide edits for completing this book. To Bonita Jewel, thank you for your invaluable editorial expertise to fi - ish the book.

Introduction

This book is about taking an inward look. It is about initiating a constructive dialogue within your mind and heart. It is about discovering the purpose for which you were created.

This book was written for those who recognize the need for understanding their identity; those who desire to see their purpose in life fulfilled.

The content is different from others in that it offers the reader practical tools to see a picture of who they desire to be and action steps to see their purpose unfold. Concise and coherent, the subject matter will appeal to the casual reader. Its depth and scope will also welcome readers who are looking for a meaningful book.

If you have found yourself wrestling with your identity because you believe that your life truly does matter, this book is for you. It is geared toward individuals trying to sort through and make sense of life, those hungry and thirsty to know the reason for their existence, those who want to engage in real talk about who they are and, just as importantly, who they can become.

So many people are dissatisfied with the results they are getting out of life because they believe there's got to be more. They simply don't know what that "more" is, or where to find it. If you feel this way, or if you desire to live at a higher level by knowing more intimately the reason you exist, I pray you will begin to find the answers within these pages. Once you discover your core purpose, you will have the ability to achieve the greatest fulfillment and results in life you have ever known.

Or perhaps you have a family member or loved one, and you would love to see them discover their purpose in life. You bear personal witness to the life they live, and you long for words to say to them that may spark a flame within their heart, awakening them to a life of purpose.

My prayer is that, as you read this book, you see it as not "just another book," but as an invitation to look at your life through the lenses of *Identification*, *Resignation*, and *Applica-*

tion (I.R.A.). What's your I.R.A.? As you read the words and grasp the ideas presented, seek points of personal identific - tion and meaning.

Identify. Look at areas in your life where you *identify* a need for a change. Perhaps it is a change in thinking. Perhaps a change in behavior.

Resign. The next step is to *resign* from activities that hin- der you from living your purpose.

Application. Finally, give attention to thought-provok- ing ideas that can be applied as you maximize your potential. Think application. That is how to get the most out of this book.

This book has been created to address the idea of your core identity, and to build and strengthen those parts that are lacking. It is to facilitate you in understanding and articulating your identity and purpose.

This book is written to ignite the possibilities of purpose within you, so that you may be encouraged to not settle for a life void of meaning, but instead pursue a life filled with an undeniable reality of significance

Embracing Your Identity and Living Your Purpose serves as a primer of sorts. It places attention on that deep concept of who we are deep inside. This question of "Who Am I?" really does matter! Where do you stand? Who are you? Do you even know?

If you desire to know your purpose and are tired of maintaining the status quo, keep reading. The following words will propel you to discovery. If you know your purpose, I welcome you to continue to read, and then pass this book on to others who are searching.

I wonder what our world would be like if every individual, every couple, every family, and every community would intentionally pursue and discover their purpose. What would life be like if there were no inhibitions to maximizing our potential?

That is something to think about, and to explore as you read. Ask yourself, "What would my life be like if I knew my true purpose? What would my days look like if I pursued my purpose with a passion? What would my world look like if I encouraged others to find and explore their unique, God-given purpose?"

If you decide that you want to live a life of fulfillme t and purpose, determine that nothing will hold you back from pursuing that deep reason God has placed in your heart. You will never regret such a decision. You will never regret such a life.

Chapter One

The Work of Purpose

Before we go any further, let us be absolutely clear about the process of pursuing our purpose. It requires work. Work is rarely sought because our physical natures seek a state of ease and comfort. Seeking after and choosing to live a God-given purpose takes a conscious choice to travel a road that few travel. This road is not always easy.

One aspect of work in regards to purpose is making a thoughtful and intentional effort to give attention to connections in life; not just any connection, but relationships that occur over a lifetime with other people and with ourselves. When we intentionally take notice of particular patterns, cycles, and circles, we might notice "life themes" becoming apparent. When we realize that certain experiences result in a deep sense of fulfillment, the work of purpose unfolds.

The work of purpose is not to be mistaken with the hard efforts in life that lead to utter frustration without results. It is recognizing who we are, and who we are to become. The process will never be a one-time event. It is a journey and not a destination. Some aspects of our life's purpose might take our entire lives to recognize or fulfill. Even when the results we desire along the road are not tangible, they can still be understood from the perspective of purpose. The work of purpose gives us the incredible ability to discover connections when there appears to be none.

There is a powerful story in the Bible that conveys this message. At the age of 17, a young man named Joseph dreamed he would someday rise to a position of leadership, and that his family would be subservient to him. His brother took great offense to this dream, as they were already jealous that Joseph was their father's favorite son.

In the process of his dream coming to pass, Joseph was thrown into a pit and sold into slavery by his brothers. He was taken to Egypt where he was purchased by a ruler, and worked in this ruler's house. Joseph did well there and caused the ruler's household to prosper. God blessed everything Joseph put his hands to. When he was falsely accused by the ruler's wife, things seemed to take a turn for the worse, as Joseph was thrown into prison. It looked like his dream would never be fulfilled. He was far from his family and in bonds once again

In prison, Joseph helped a couple of inmates by interpreting their dreams. Afterwards, one of the men promised that he would remember Joseph after getting out of jail. The man was restored to his place as wine bearer to the king, but Joseph remained in prison for another two years, as the man forgot his promise.

One day, the pharaoh of Egypt had a dream that troubled him deeply and no one could understand the meaning of this dream. The wine bearer remembered Joseph and shared Joseph's talent of interpreting dreams with the king of Egypt. Joseph was called to interpret the king's dream. When brought before the greatest man in Egypt and asked if he could interpret dreams, he humbly answered, "It is not in me; God will give Pharaoh an answer" (Gen. 41:16). God did give Pharaoh an answer through Joseph, as he interpreted the dream. Through this, Joseph's dream was also answered. He was promoted to second in command of all of Egypt. Eventually, his family also moved to Egypt and lived under Joseph's leadership.

The work of purpose in Joseph's life took 13 years to come to fruition. When Joseph was reunited with his brothers, they begged forgiveness as they feared for their lives. The little brother was now the second most powerful person in the land. But Joseph was able to see the big picture of all the events that had taken place in his life. Thrown into the pit, sold into slavery, working in the palace, being falsely accused and thrown into prison – Joseph understood these events in relationship to a larger purpose. It took all these for him to arrive in Egypt and be in a place where he could foretell a time of famine – not only to save the lives of the Egyptians, but to save the life of his family, through which line would eventually come the Savior of the world: Jesus, the Christ.

One event connected to another, enabling Joseph to understand and fulfill his purpose in life. He might not have understood the entire scope, but his confidence in God's plan gave him faith and peace in the midst of difficult .

Like Joseph, we must seek to grasp the idea of the work of purpose. It will allow us to climb above a moment, an event, or an experience to obtain or reestablish the big picture of life. Challenging experiences and difficult events are not the sum total of our potential. Seeing the big picture of our lives allows us an opportunity to remain steady in the process of living out whom we are born to be. Recognizing the connections between our past, present, and future can fill our hearts with faith in the midst of trial, and confidence in God s ultimate plan.

What is in your big picture? See yourself in the picture because you know your identity and have the faith that you can fulfill your purpose. Take the challenge and give it a try!

The Ingredient of Work

Now that we understand the often-overlooked reality about the ongoing work of purpose, let's get to work. God works His purpose, yes, but it requires *our* work in addition to His. Big dreams, giant-sized visions, and lofty goals do not occur in a vacuum. They require high levels of commitment that will sustain us as we journey through the maze of realizing our greatest potential.

If you have read up to this point and are enthusiastic about the prospects before you, I believe that you not only have what it takes to overcome every obstacle standing in the way of realizing your purpose, but perhaps you are also ready to *live* at the next level. Pursuing purpose is not a one-time decision; it is a lifestyle.

Personal characteristics like passion, desire, hunger, thirst, and discontentment are surefire attributes that can catapult you into your destiny, depending on how you respond to them. The characteristics listed above are not academic lessons to be learned in a classroom or from a textbook. They are attributes born from within. A passion to discover your purpose is the spark that lights a flame in your soul. A desire to pursue that purpose is the life to keep going forward. Inner hunger can serve as the necessary fervor you need to accomplish the process of living out your God-given purpose. Spiritual thirst can keep you anchored to the Source of all strength and power. Finally, a measure of discontentment at your current state of living or spirituality can propel you on the path of living out your deeply-felt purpose.

At the same time, each of these characteristics require a response from us. They require *work*. Opportunities are often forfeited or missed in life because of an unwillingness to apply a sound work ethic to the process. We must take up the challenge and take active steps forward. Opportunities will rarely be handed to us on the proverbial silver platter.

A great question to ask yourself is, "Am I ready to take the challenge of relentlessly pursuing what I have been born to do?" Demand of yourself a response, and do not let it be a shallow, surface-level reply. Yes, you may be a good singer, writer, dancer, deal maker, nurse, politician, accountant, or business owner, but is this what you were *born* to do? Is this the deep calling God has given you?

The Purpose for Purpose

Why do we need to discover our purpose?

What does purpose even mean? The Encarta dictionary describes purpose as "the reason for which something exists or for which it has been done or made" (reason for existence); "the goal or intended outcome of something" (desired effect); and lastly, "the desire or the resolve necessary to accomplish a goal" (determination).

Nothing in life brings more confusion than something or someone being used for reasons other than its purpose. Think of any machine or piece of equipment. You wouldn't use a blender to cook your food; nor would you use an oven to store your food. You would use those utilities for their specific purpose. It is the same with us!

Our expectations of ourselves will be met with continuous frustration when those expectations are not in alignment with who we were born to be and what we are born to do. Our expectations of others will suffer a similar fate. If we have any reasonable amount of speculation that there is more to life than what we are currently experiencing, we can never completely settle for less than optimal results. Even if we do nothing about this feeling, deep down in our heart of hearts lies a discontentment screaming for an exit. No other inner calling is like the call for purpose and reason for being. Although as humans we may at times act like we have given up, each of us bear a deep wellspring of hope that life can be lived with greater levels of significance.

The need for discovering our purpose is not something that originates from without, but is conceptualized from within. Some call it a hunch. Some label it as a gut-level wonderment. Others describe it as personal intuition. Whatever we call our "it," something inside us yearns for the truth of knowing and living out our reason for being on earth.

Whether the world acknowledges your significance or not, you do matter. You are worth so much more than you might recognize or see at the moment. The realization of our identity is a process that must be developed from within. As we tap into the hidden treasures of our humanity, we will begin to recognize these threads of purpose and meaning. The "living your purpose" journey begins with recognizing and embracing your identity – who you are and who you can become.

How can you recognize this inner calling of purpose? If you are dissatisfied with your place of employment, purpose is calling. If you are disappointed with your educational progress, purpose is calling. If you are displeased with your interpersonal relationship with your spouse, your family, or your friends because they lack fulfillm nt, purpose is calling. If you are fed up with the monkey of lack on your back, or tired of being broke and in debt, purpose is calling. If you are a millionaire and all your bills are paid, yet you are mentally, emotionally, and spiritually bankrupt, purpose is calling.

Purpose can pursue you, no matter who you are or where you stand in life. If you are a CEO, a multimillion-dollar athlete, a Hollywood star, a news anchor, an elected official, an educator, a mental health professional, a stay-at-home mom or dad, a recent high school or college graduate, a small or mega-church pastor, a military service member, a veteran of the Armed Forces, or a person of any other status, but have no quality of life, *purpose is calling.*

It does not matter what position or title you hold. If you lack fulfillm nt, passion, or a sense of maximizing your potential, the voice of purpose cries out to be discovered, nurtured, and lived.

Every individual in life needs to not only have a sense of purpose, but needs to also intentionally make choices in life directly related to achieving a life that matters and makes a difference. Such intentional living truly will make a difference in this world.

I am intrigued by the fact no two *fingerprint* are the same. Everything about us is unique – our DNA, our upbringing, our thoughts, our individual hopes, dreams, and perspectives. Although we are physically unique, we often tend to copycat the lives of others. As such, we rarely tap into the wealth of difference that lies within us. We are often given instructions by our culture or upbringing on what to wear, how to talk, what to think, where to live, what career to choose, who to look like, who to work for, and other ideas on what to do and how to do it in order to have a successful life.

Bob Buford, in his book *Halftime*, discusses a pivotal mid-life phenomenon where people wrestle with the decision to move from a life of *success* to a life of *significanc* . He observes that the first half of our lives are often spent trying to achieve a certain level of success. Then, sometimes almost too late it seems, we discover an inner desire for a more meaningful life. We begin to ask encompassing questions such as, "Does my life matter? What can I do that will make a lasting difference? Is it too late to try?"

I believe we often encounter these phases in life when little focus is placed on the importance of living a life of purpose and significance from an early age. I do not recall any classes during my entire educational life that covered the necessity of living a life of purpose and how it will contribute to a productive and fulfilling life. Even in my undergraduate and graduate work, classes on purpose were not available.

Every educational institution – from preschools to doctoral

programs – could contribute to student success in their personal and professional lives by providing an entry-level course entitled "Life Purpose 101." While the goal of the class would not be to tell students exactly what they should do with their lives, it could serve to encourage thinking about and connecting with life in terms of purpose.

Imagine your son or daughter viewing life according to their God-ordained purpose and having enthusiasm about the possibilities of who they can become. A young person realizing purpose could mean the difference between successful completion of high school, college, entrepreneurial endeavors, and other meaningful career pursuits … or falling by the wayside by dropping out and living life short of their full potential.

Likewise, adults who have journeyed through life without mentorship on the importance of living one's purpose could benefit from a "Life Purpose 101" course – regardless of age, experience, or background. As long as there is breath in your body and the mental capacity to desire a productive life, it is not too late! I have personally witnessed adults in their late

50s and 60s start and complete graduate-level degrees. On the day of pomp and circumstance, they proudly walked across the stage and received their diplomas, matched by a standing ovation all over the auditorium.

After seeing adults later in life achieve their long-anticipated educational goals, I could not help but to be inspired, motivated, and challenged to look within and ask the questions: "What is my purpose in life? What am I doing to fulfill it? Am I doing all I can to be all I can be?"

We would all do well to ask ourselves those thoughts regularly. You may be thinking your situation may be an exception, but I want to encourage you again, "It's not too late!"

Let's take a mental "joy ride" for a moment. Imagine your life without those hang-ups that continually get in the way of pursuing your dreams. Picture yourself doing what you were born to do and being who you aspire to be. Envision an existence loaded with contentment because you are living your purpose.

Living your purpose is not a one-time occasion, but a process of discovery. While in the course of discovery, new meaning and development of purpose can materialize and continually propel us towards the core of who we are created to be. Without a mental map, it is difficult to visualize the future we want. Our ability to see the future we desire to see is linked to a healthy view and embracing of our unique identity.

Embracing and Pursuing for International Change

(E.P.I.C.)

At some point in an individual's life, a deep cry from within calls for a life that is meaningful and significant. Living a life that matters is a part of human existence.

As a young boy all the way into my pre-adolescent years, I desired to become a professional basketball player. My favorite player at the time was Julius Erving, known as "Dr. J." Oh, how I admired Dr. J's ability to perform on the basketball court with such skill, grace, and mind-blowing moves. I wanted to be just like him. Throughout most of my youth, I grew up in a rural South Georgia and spent many hours trying to develop my basketball skills. Most of the time, all I had was a dirt basketball court and a goal my mother brought for my brother and me. I practiced and I practiced, as hard and as much as I could, to make my dream of making it to the NBA become a reality. This dream continued through my teen years. I played basketball every year in high school. By the time I became a senior, I realized that my dream of playing in the NBA was not materializing on the court. Although I played other sports – football, baseball, and track – and I was good at them, my heart's desire was to play basketball. A life that mattered for me during my youth was to play basketball at the next level. It didn't matter to me that I had scholarship offers to play football at the college level; I wanted to play *basketball*.

Needless to say, basketball beyond high school was not a part of my eventual path in life. It was not until years later that I realized the deep cry from within during my early years was not, in fact, specifically to join the NBA. My soul was calling out for a life of significance and a life that mattered. While my focus throughout my youth was on playing a sport, the process of identifying my purpose had begun. Sometimes we can have a passion for doing one thing, or even a number of things, but that pursuit may not be our *purpose*.

After talking with a friend about my story of high interest in sports, but low interest in education, I discovered something else. Instead of being a student-athlete; I was an athlete-student. Playing sports was more important to me than getting an education. Yes, I had purpose, but it was not balanced with a priority on learning. I did not see academic studies as an important part of my purpose. I graduated, but had to catch up later in life.

I can only imagine the untold stories of young people like myself who have grown up, or are growing up now, longing to do something in life that really matters to them. Longing to be someone who matters to *others*. I can only imagine the innumerable dreams in the hearts of young people and adults longing after a deeper reality than the one they are living. They only lack the guidance and mentorship to follow a path leading to a life of worth. A pattern of embracing one's identity and living a life of purpose is needed as early in life as possible.

What would happen if we had systematic life-purpose processes in our public, private, and family educational systems to help our youth discover who they were born to be? Even if a person has grown beyond their youth, they could also benefit from intentionally focusing on embracing their identity and living their purpose. While this focus is not in place, we would do well by starting with *ourselves* and others upon whom we have influence.

When attempting to grasp the reality of our purpose, two key actions are necessary to move us from where we are to where our Creator designed us to be.

First, we must *embrace* our God-given uniqueness that cannot be duplicated by another or surrendered to the identity of another. Whenever we lose our sense of identity, it is at our own expense, and often to our own peril. We literally rob ourselves and the world of the privilege of getting to know the genuine creation that we are.

There are some things about our lives that are similar to others; yet there are aspects of ourselves that set us apart from others. What sets us apart from others is God's picture of who we are. The depiction God gives us is born of a supernatural quality; this gift of God makes possible those things that we are unable to do on our own. The impossible becomes possible in that our God-given identity is derived from the very nature of God.

The book of Judges speaks to this in the story of Gideon. Chapter 6, verse 12 says, *"An angel of the Lord appeared to Gideon,"* and said, *"The Lord is with you, mighty warrior"* (NIV). Later Gideon is told, *"Go in this strength you have and save Israel out of Midian's hand"* (Judges 6:14). At the time the angel gave this description of Gideon, his reality looked nothing like a "mighty warrior." The Israelite community, whom Gideon was a part of, was oppressed by the Midianites. The people were living in mountain clefts, caves, and other places to hide from their oppressors.

The oppression of Israel trickled down to Gideon's perception of his clan as well as how he viewed himself. Gideon said, *"My clan is the weakest in Manasseh, and I am the least in my family*" (Judges 6:15b). In spite of this, Gideon was called "mighty warrior." Gideon's reality had to catch up with God's reality of who he was. God's description of who we are often creates tension because sometimes our circumstances do not reflect our true selves. In this example, we find Gideon searching for a fit with his present condition and God's vision of him as a "mighty warrior." In other words, Gideon struggled with embracing his God-given identity.

The word "embrace" means to hold someone or something closely in one's arms. Embrace also means to accept or support a belief, theory, or change willingly or enthusiastically. With a history like Gideon's, it makes sense that it was difficult for him to hold or accept willingly and enthusiastically a new name divinely given to him. The very thought was quite distant from his current reality.

Not unlike Gideon, we often find ourselves wrestling with self-described displeasure of self, versus embracing the revelation of being made in the image of God. Grasping God's view of ourselves is fundamental to understanding who we are and living a life filled with possibilities to achieve our greatest potential.

While embracing our God-given identity is important, complementary to it is the action of *pursuing*. Pursue means to chase, to run after, to follow someone or something in order to catch, or to continue or proceed along a path or route. It is not enough to just embrace our identity, but by any means necessary, we must give relentless attention to understanding and developing our identity.

Pursuing involves the realization that, "Who I am to become, I already am." God has already given you the abilities, talents, and gifts that you need. All that is remaining is for you to claim it in active faith, living out the reality of your God-ordained potential. As we live our lives, it is important to know our identity is not somewhere "out there." It is a seed already planted within you, needing to be believed, nourished, and cultivated for its unique greatness. The action of pursuit is not an endless chase after the unknown, but a process of becoming one with and accepting who we were born to be.

The act of pursuing does not mean we have all the answers. It means that we humbly embrace the reality that there is more inside of us that needs to be developed in order to meet the possibilities of our God-given purpose.

I make use of the tag "Embrace and Pursue for International Change" (E.P.I.C.) as a metaphor for creating the language and vision necessary to see life beyond ourselves. Our world becomes a better place when we connect to the epicenter of our being and recognize within that center a design for a life of positive impact. One does not have to be an international traveler in order to change the world. Grasping our identity and having a strong sense of purpose enables us to experience a change of our world *within*, which increases our capacity to influence the world within our reach.

International change is a way of describing the unlimited possibilities as we embrace a lifestyle of passionate purpose. If you are serious about your desire to know your purpose, mark this day as a day of change, personal positioning for greater clarity, and freedom to be who you are created to be. If you find yourself timid, apprehensive, or reluctant about moving forward in your life, a new beginning is now possible as you embark upon the reality of your identity. Embracing a new beginning and setting out on this path toward a life of purpose is a key process that will facilitate sound reasons to pursue who you were born to be. Determine that this will be the day you embrace your core identity. Let the Spirit of God speak to your heart and inspire within you the picture of who God created you to be.

Overcoming Anxiety in Embracing Identity

E.P.I.C. endeavors that are worth pursuing are often accompanied by strong and potentially paralyzing emotions. God might desire to implant a dream within you, but this dream is often met with the natural reactions of emotions such as fear, intimidation, inferiority, rejection, anxiety, and the sense that who you are is not enough. The anxiety that builds up due to these emotions can drive you to relentless pursuits to gain acceptance or approval of others.

Such empty pursuits often come hand in hand with the feeling that others are superior to you somehow. With this mindset, negative thought patterns can start to develop. These include being overly concerned with how others feel about you and what others think about you. If not recognized and broken, the mentality of seeking the approval of others begin to cement in your mind, further paralyzing you from pursuing your God-given destiny.

When our minds are ensnared with the burden of what other people think about us, we function out of a deficit mentality. This mentality focuses on the perception that "who I am is not enough," and there is a discrepancy between whom we are and who we perceive ourselves to be. In the deficit mode of thought, our relationships with others and even with ourselves are driven by overwhelming feelings of uneasiness about our identity. Standing up for what we really believe in is difficult because so much energy is placed in the debilitating belief that other people's opinions and behaviors are more valuable than our own. Instead of speaking up and addressing issues in life based on our core beliefs, we then make decisions with worry of being rejected by others.

With this deficit mentality, our identity is wrapped in the character and reactions of others. When we experience anxiety and start questioning the legitimacy of who we are, a message being communicated at the gut level is that the foundation of who we are cannot be trusted. Perhaps you can think of times in your life when you stopped to think about how you behaved with someone else, and you wished you had responded differently. If we look closely at our behavior, we may find a pattern of similar situations when we respond and later regret that response. We ask ourselves questions like: "Why didn't I just speak up when I had the chance? Would the outcome be different if I had followed my mind? Why was I afraid so that I didn't do anything?"

When interacting with others, anxiety can get in the way of our being true to ourselves and true to the person God has created us to be. Anxiety can incite our attention toward pacifying the whims and desires of others. How can we break out of this paralyzing mindset?

It is extremely important to see yourself as approved by God to be 100% *you*. In being you, there is no competition, no need for approval, no fear of rejection or invalidation. When you are yourself, no one can compete because no one can compare with you. Stand, live, perform, work, think, be, present, lead, and follow as one approved by God, and deeply loved by God. Your existence as authorized by your Creator has already been validated, confirmed, and cleared.

Get a Mental Picture of Your Approval

One action that is paramount is getting a mental picture of ourselves approved by our Creator. This picture will render us whole, complete, and enough. It will enable us to envision ourselves possessing the goods, having what it takes, and distinct from everyone else. When you develop this Godly perception of yourself, you will understand that no one can beat you at being you.

There's a story about a bear walking around in a kitten skin costume, pretending to be a kitten. Everywhere the bear went, the bear presented itself as a kitten. In greeting other animals in the forest, the bear would say, "Meow!" The bear met the fox, the deer, and the moose and told them he was a kitten. He even introduced himself to other bears as a kitten. He did this to scores of other animals in the forest.

Some responded cautiously with suspicion about who this creature really was, but kept quiet. Others embraced the bear as he had introduced himself and they treated the bear as a kitten. None of the animals had the courage to let the bear know he was different, and that it was okay to be different because they knew that the bear loved pretending to be a kitten.

One day, the bear was walking along in the woods and met a wise turtle by a stream of water. This turtle had been living in the forest for a very long time and knew the name and identity of every animal in the forest.

The bear said, "Hello, turtle."

The wise turtle said, "Hello, bear."

The bear responded with dismay and shock that the wise turtle did not identify him correctly. "Pardon me," said the bear-kitten, "I am a kitten."

The wise turtle responded, "Oh, no, you may have disguised yourself as a kitten and have the presentation of a kitten, but you are certainly no kitten. You are a bear."

"Oh, no," said the bear, "you are wrong. I can't be a bear because all my life I have been a kitten and no one else told me otherwise."

The wise turtle responded, "It's time for you to get a picture of who you really are." "Come with me near the stream," said the wise turtle. And they slowly moved toward the stream at the pace of the wise turtle.

While on the way, the bear-kitten was approaching the stream with doubt and disbelief that he could be anything other than a kitten. After getting to the stream, the wise turtle said to the bear-kitten, "Now take a look in the stream and tell me what you see."

The bear-kitten looked and said, "I am looking and all I see is the water I drink every day." And the bear-kitten, being thirsty, began drinking water from the stream.

The wise turtle sternly told the bear-kitten, "Lift your head up and look again. This time hold still and look not at the water, but look at the reflection from the water and tell me what you see."

The bear-kitten said, "This can't be right. I see a bear." The bear-kitten looked around to see if there was another bear behind, but found no one.

The bear-kitten looked in the stream again and the wise turtle asked the bear-kitten, "Now this time tell me WHO you see?"

The bear-kitten responded with more clarity and belief than ever before, "I see a bear and that bear is me. I am not a kitten." The bear roared with a loud bear roar and never meowed again.

The bear went back to his old circle of animal friends a changed creature, and from that time on, the bear lived as a bear. Some of his friends were disappointed because bear had discovered his identity and they distanced themselves from the bear. Others embraced and celebrated the bear's true identity. More important than any of the other animals' responses, the bear accepted the reality of WHO he was and no longer attempted to live like a kitten, even if that meant living alone.

If we are going to embrace our identity and live our purpose, we need to get a picture of WHO we really are. Go to a spot, a pond, a stream, or a pool of water (and yes, be careful not to fall in). Look and see your reflection in the water. Your physical attributes will be reflected in the water. Whatever you look like, like it or not, it is you!

Take your hand and wave it across the top of the water to erase your reflection. Whenever the water settles, you will discover your reflection has not changed. You are still you! Like waving the water away cannot change your physical appearance, trying to be someone who you are not, does not change WHO you were created to be.

We must learn to accept who we are, both externally and internally. We live in a society that can be cruel on someone's appearance if it is not the accepted look. People pay millions of dollars to adjust their physical body in order to fit a personal, societal, or professional norm or expectation. We could spend a lifetime fighting against WHO we really are and never learn to embrace our current realities as a starting point for change.

If you do not like WHERE you are in life, do not confuse it with WHO you are. If we discover WHO we are, knowing our identity can positively impact WHERE we are. In being true to ourselves, we will take actions to improve our current place in life based on WHO we are at the core.

Having a mature understanding of the negative role anxiety can play and the impact it may have on our relationships can help us be aware of this trap. Refusing to allow anxiety to have a place in our lives will assist us in embracing who we are more fully.

No matter who you are or where you find yourself in life, the importance of embracing the reality of your identity cannot be underscored enough. Who you are matters! Your uniqueness is a treasure to the world, just as you are a treasure to the God who created you.

Settling the Issues with Our Identity

Embracing our identity among *self, family of origin, marriage and family life, work life, and other relationships* is needed for us to bring about E.P.I.C. change. First and foremost, we need to be settled within *ourselves* concerning who we are. Settling inner conflict with our identity makes it possible to de-velop balanced and healthy relationships with others. If we are going to have healthy relationships with others, we must first begin to relate to ourselves with dignity and respect.

You have likely heard many stories about bullying in local schools or on the playground. Often, the perpetrator has not come to realize and accept his or her identity as valuable and significant. The issue of self-identity has not been settled in the life of a bully. What's interesting about bullying is that it can take place in different types of relationships, not only in school and on the playground. Bullying can take place in the work environment, in politics, with sports, among family, and on social media to name a few. When there is any form of in-timidation, mistreatment, oppression, harassment or hounding of others – and this includes maltreatment of ourselves – it's often done out of unsettled issues with identity.

Settling the issue of identity with our *family of origin* is also important. Your family of origin is the family who raised you. It is the place you learned the basics of how you see yourself and how you see the world. As such, your family had a significant amount of influence regarding values you learned during your formative years. You had no decision-making authority about who your family of origin would be. If your experiences with your family of origin have not been good, the memories of those experiences can be extremely painful and become a potential barrier to discovering your identity. Your sense of self or level of self-esteem might have been severely harmed due to an abusive or dysfunctional background.

But at an even deeper level, you are not your family. In a curious and respectful manner, a very wise son said to his parents, "I want to know who I am *apart from my family*." While growing up to young adulthood, this young man lived his life under the identity of his family. But along the way, his interest grew into knowing who he was outside of his family.

First, he had to settle the issue that he was in fact a product of his family of origin.

Second, he discovered he had distinct qualities that gave him his own identity. These qualities provided a gateway for him to live his life. He made the decision to own his past. He refused to let it sabotage his present and future ability to be all he could be.

Settling the issue of identity in *marriage and family* is an-other external relationship that hinges on how well we relate to self. When two people come together in marriage, having a strong sense of self-identity will enable the union to grow and become strong. The idea of a healthy marriage is two people who unite with a healthy mindset about the need for interde-pendence in marriage. Interdependence in marriage is the idea of accepting and meeting each other's need for mutual support and individuality in the relationship.

When the two unite as one, they have the opportunity to become interdependent. There should be some healthy levels of dependence in marriage where couples rely upon each other for support and being responsible for certain areas in the mar-riage (i.e. work, budgeting, communication, problem-solving, etc.). There should also be a healthy sense of *in*dependence where one spouse is not swallowed up in the other to the point of losing his or her identity. If a spouse is not able to think and speak independently of the other, this is a sign of unhealthy dependence.

Settling the issue of one's identity in marriage and family will prepare the foundation for a very happy, stable, and enduring home. Reaching a healthy state of interdependence within a marriage can be a challenge, yet it is worth the effort.

Settling the issue of identity in *work life and other relationships* carries the same principles as the previous relationships, even though they have different contexts. We need to know who we are in our work life. We are not paid to sort out our identity at work. The best companies, the best organizations, the best teams, and the best performers in the marketplace are those who understand who they are and their role in the orga-nization.

A strong sense of self in one's professional work life gives companies the best resources to understand, embrace, and carry out the goals and objectives of the organization. Settling the issue of identity in work life establishes a foundation for not allowing personal feelings to get in the way of a professional focus on job-related tasks.

Settling the issues of identity in each of these areas is imperative. We can only get the best results out of life when we understand WHO we are. Regardless of the environment we are in, the uniqueness of our design can flourish rather than be diminished in the face of pressure to conform and be like someone else. This strength is borne of knowing one's God-given purpose and core identity.

When considering these factors, our E.P.I.C is at stake. We have the opportunity to Embrace and Pursue our Purpose for International Change. Our E.P.I.C. is not as much about a geographical location as it is about understanding our identity, our purpose, and being the best we can be anytime, anyplace, and anywhere – impacting change for the good.

If as you read this last section, you found a growing awareness of a need for change in your family, marriage, or work life, take some time to prayerfully consider how you can develop a healthy balance of awareness, identity, and interdependence. Ask God to help you grow in the areas you feel might be lacking, and in all you do, seek to pursue a greater purpose.

Explore points of I.R.A. as you reflect on Chapter One and use the space provided to write areas of:

Identification – Look at areas in your life where you *identify* a need for a change. Thinking? Behavior?

Resignation – *Resign* from activities that hinder you from living your purpose.

Application – Ideas that can be *applied* as you maximize your potential. Think *application*.

Chapter Two

Five Reasons to Pursue Purpose
(Don't Leave Earth without It!)

Reason # 1: Purpose Ignites Vision!

Some of the most frustrating and unfulfilled times in my life have been periods where I did not have a clear picture about where I was headed. Simply beginning a day without direction or goals to accomplish that day can lead toward paths of unproductive living. At the same time, even with a productive schedule of waking up, going to work, leaving work, and coming back home, purpose can become lost in the daily routine of the work-home life cycle. We can become so familiar with our regular daily activities that we lose sight of the possibilities of greater fulfillment in life.

When this phenomenon occurs in my life, I discover that more often than not, I lack a sense of purpose. Anywhere or anytime there is a lack of purpose – relational or organizational – chaos, confusion, frustration, ineffectiveness, lack of productivity, or poor quality of life may occur. At such times, I find that I need to stop, refocus, and find my center. Usually the first place to look, and the best place, is in the Word of God.

Webster's Dictionary defines the noun "purpose" as "something set up as an object or end to be attained" and as an "intention." As a verb, "purpose" is described by Webster's as "a subject under discussion or an action in the course of execution." Purpose then, involves focus on a specific target and includes corresponding actions taken to achieve desired goals.

A reflective question we might regularly ask is, "Am I in execution of my purpose? If so, how am I doing so?" In order to live out our purpose in life, focus and action are required.

A sobering example from Proverbs 29:18 tells us, "Where there is no vision, the people perish" (KJV). Another translation states, "Where there is no revelation, the people cast off restraint" (NIV). Without a vision, people tend to cast off restraint. When this occurs, the ability to maintain boundaries in life are underdeveloped, goal achievement is compromised, and success is often aborted. When there is no intentional focus and actions to match the focus, the fruit that follows is a misguided life without fulfillment. In other words, life can run wild and veer from its intended course.

When purpose is present and realized, a vision for life is ignited. Purpose provides a metaphoric North Star that shines day or night and has the ability to guide through fog, rain, snow, and places of low visibility. In the midst of the difficu - ties we face on a regular basis, purpose gives us the ability to "see in the dark."

Purpose has the likeness of a magnet, too. Though we may be in the dark and cannot see our way through, the magnetic pull of purpose supernaturally assists us with navigating through trials, hardships, and the seemingly insurmountable difficulties of life. Like a compass, purpose can serve as a Magnetic North. When we find ourselves without direction, lacking hope, lost, or uncertain about where to turn, our God-given purpose tells us which way is north. It helps us to re-establish a path of a meaningful life.

In search for meaning, purpose becomes our light switch, enabling us to see and thus regain our ability to focus or re-focus when we have drifted off course. As the fire of purpose ignites our vision, we are motivated to live out what we see. Our God-ordained vision helps create a brighter future.

Reason # 2: Purpose Influences Motivation

It is 10 o'clock at night and the possibility of a new day is on the horizon. What are *you* doing? A person with a strong sense that their life has purpose and meaning tucks in for the night to rest in preparation and expectation for what a new day might bring. The motivation to prepare for the next day is driven by the individual's awareness of a purposed life. She may not be able to fully articulate it, but knows there's more to her life than what is happening at the moment. Knowing our purpose can provide the necessary spark for a sustained life of fulfillment

Within each one of us lies the potential to achieve greatness. This greatness is often first conceptualized through some
sort of a mental picture, which can take form through dreams,
visions, observations of nature and people, and numerous other methods. Having a picture of a goal or a desired result helps
us facilitate and sustain the motivation we need to achieve a
desired end. Motivation is a necessary internal quality we must
maintain if we truly endeavor to see our dreams and goals become reality.

Answers to the question of what motivates our behavior or
particular actions can be quite elusive. Why do we do what we
do? What makes us tick? What makes some people respond in
certain ways, and other people in a completely different way?

These questions and other quests for understanding human
behavior take concerted time and effort to understand. David
Edwards, author of *Motivation and Emotion: Evolutionary,
Physiological, Cognitive, and Social Influence* , uses words
such as "energy" and "vitality" in describing what motivation
is. When we lack energy, drive, and passion for any endeavor,

goal attainment may seem virtually impossible. On the flip side, with purpose, the seemingly impossible can become possible. This occurs because the desired end is matched with the motivation needed to get the job done.

Motivation is linked to our ability to thrive in life. When we lack motivation, anything and everything becomes difficult to do. Life itself becomes a bore and a chore. Purpose fuels our motivation to keep going when tempted to give up on our goals, dreams, or worthwhile pursuits. The "why" of life calls for energy and vitality needed to keep going, to keep trying, to keep fighting, to keep hoping, and patiently waiting and working toward the fulfillment of your dreams.

If you feel that your days are void of hope and possibility, try to include the realization of connecting to your purpose. This one "missing link" can ultimately produce the motivation you need to achieve a life of fulfillment and unparalleled success.

Having a sense of purpose not only influences motivation, but can also serve as a wisdom-producing agent for change and progress as we move towards fulfilling our goals. The wisdom of purpose helps us to distinguish between a feelings-based life and a principle-based life.

A feelings-based life is when our decision making is determined by our emotional state. Those who live a feeling-based life will use their emotions as their guideposts for making decisions. Anger, sadness, anxiety, or happiness will be the hinge upon which minor and major issues are determined.

As humans, we can experience a range of emotions in any given period of our lives. If our decision making is centered on how we feel, our lives will be riddled with indecisiveness and duplicity. James, a New Testament writer, alludes to this reality when he notes, "a double-minded man is unstable in all his ways" (James 1:8). While it is important to be in touch with how we feel and to acknowledge and validate our emotions, making feelings-based decisions can lead us on a path of instability and utter chaos. Our lives will be chaotic because of the very nature of feelings; they come and they go. As such, emotions require the compliment of balanced thinking, especially when it comes to making decisions.

A principle-based life is one that is governed by decision making based on core principles and deeply-held values. Principles, unlike emotions, are constant and reliable rules for life. Because they do not fluctuate, principles can be a solid foundation for making decisions, especially difficult ones.

Making principle-based decisions can be tough because the emotions we experience can be powerful and overwhelming. Yet, the wisdom of purpose can assist us in giving attention to core principles for living and enable us to remain on track with achieving our goals. In essence, a strong sense of purpose empowers us to make decisions that are in alignment with the results we want to see.

When our focus is in sync with our purpose and what we desire to see, we obtain motivation to continue the journey. Having a sense of purpose can be a lifeline to the enduring motivation needed to get the job done. Motivation and purpose are inextricably connected.

I remember during my military days how important it was

for a new recruit to have the goal of graduating from basic training. This motivational tool was vital for successful completion of the course. In order for me to personally accomplish this, I had to see myself among my graduating class marching on the parade field, being recognized for finishing the course. It was important for me to have a vision of the end from the beginning. When the challenge of physical training, learning my general orders, marksmanship, and other battlefie d tactics tempted to make my resolve waver, the *purpose* of graduating served as a motivating factor to dig deep, push through the pain, and finish strong.

My drill sergeant would ask a very important question: "Are you motivated?"

I, along with other soldiers, would respond, "Motivated, motivated, drill sergeant!"

When motivation is present to help us do what needs to be done, the reality of attaining our purpose can come into focus. Although my goal was to finish basic training, I needed motivation to complete the individual tasks along the way. In this instance, the purpose of graduation fueled my motivation to focus and achieve my goal. When purpose is accompanied by motivation, we strengthen our ability to hang in there until our desired future is achieved.

It is important to understand that pursuing our purpose is a process of a lifetime. As mentioned earlier, it is not a one-time event. So then what enables us to continue with the process when we do not see fulfillment in a day, a week, a year, or ten years? Motivation is the key necessary for sustaining our ability to focus on becoming the best we can be. In noting one of Mahatma Ghandhi's top ten fundamentals for changing the world, Henrik Edberg highlighted the idea of being persistent. Edberg added, "When you find out what you really like to do, then you will discover the motivation needed to keep you going."

Sometimes we try to discover deep or mysterious answers to simple problems of not getting what we want out of life. Quite often, the struggle is attached to low motivation. While there are other factors that are relevant to fulfilling our purpose, we must not neglect the motivation factor. It is frequently the primary element missing from actively pursuing a life of purpose.

The wisdom writer of the Bible, King Solomon, esteems the impact of a person's physical hunger in a compelling and brilliant manner. Solomon declared in one of his proverbs, "The laborer's appetite works for him and his hunger drives him on" (Proverbs 16:26). Purpose void of appetite to see it through leads to a life of emptiness and discontentment.

Understanding and knowing our purpose must be met by an unparalleled desire to keep pursuing meaning and fulfil - ment even when we feel like giving up and hopelessness lurks on the horizon. Having the hunger to fulfill your purpose keeps the motor running and the wheels turning for positive move- ment towards your goal.

What are you hungry for in life?

Are you hungry enough to do what it takes to reach your goal? Oftentimes, the difference between the lives we envision for ourselves and our current realities are a matter of hunger.

How bad do you want it?

Once, I was challenged by a mentor regarding a career path in my life because he noticed a pattern of procrastination in completing the necessary tasks to be successful. He raised a thought-provoking comment about my efforts, saying, "Maybe you don't like what you are doing and you are trying to live out the expectations that others have placed on you."

He was right. I recognized at that moment it was not enough to do what others expected of me. If it was not connected to who I really was and what I truly desired to do and be in life, the appetite of my efforts would eventually ebb. My own inner hunger would not be driving me forward, and without that get-up-and-go, my career would ultimately fail.

Sometimes we do not have the hunger necessary for completing works or projects due to transferred purpose. This purpose transfer occurs when, somewhere along the course of life, the purpose of another is taken on by us. We might not even realize that we are living the life of someone else, a life that is not for us.

In our upbringing and society, we are sometimes trained on how to be like others. The underlying issue of trying to live vicariously through the lives of others can sometimes lie dor-mant without our knowing. The result is living out an identity that is not our own. A bear is a bear. A cat is a cat. No amount of "meowing" will change that.

You are *you*. You are worth taking the time to intentionally pursue and live out the greatness within you. When we begin to understand that we have an identity like no other person, the hunger or appetite necessary to live our purpose will not be too far away.

When considering the element of motivation, these two questions might prove helpful:

First, "Is my lack of motivation related to my need to take a break to replenish myself and then continue my current course?"

Second, "Is my lack of motivation connected with a hard-to-face reality that I have absolutely no passion to do what I am doing?"

The reason we must start with the first question is that sometimes the difference between high and low levels of motivation is a good night's rest or time off that will allow us to be refreshed physically, mentally, emotionally, spiritually, and socially. It may not be that we are on the wrong track, but that we just need some good ol' fashion rest and relaxation.

The reason we must also ask the second question is that if we are not on a course in alignment with our passion, no amount of rest will cure passionless pursuits. At some point, our fire will eventually go out. This is why a deeply-felt purpose and a passion to pursue it is extremely vital.

Reason # 3: Purpose Introduces Us to Untapped Potential

One of the most amazing qualities about our humanity is that there is something exceptional within all of us. Whether we recognize it or not, this unique potential exists. Whether we embrace it or not, we cannot deny it. Experiences we have had in our lives can sometimes cover up the untapped potential within us, yet it remains like a well of deep water that has not yet been discovered.

When a child is born, the child does not have the power to choose his family. At the same time, like cookie dough that has been placed in a pan for baking, the ingredients of that child have already been set. What's in you – whether known or not – is in you. Many times, we live unaware of the areas of our lives that lie dormant and undiscovered. This untapped potential within us is simply waiting. Sometimes the untapped only needs a gentle nudge to get us going and awaken to us a deeper meaning in life.

Connecting to our God-given purpose facilitates a "tapping process" that helps us to uncover inner strengths and value. Identifying our purpose helps us to narrow our focus and aids in decision-making. It helps us put our futures in alignment with our agreed-upon goals.

Tapping the well of life within enables us to realize the dreams we thought were impossible. Many people look outside of themselves for the deep answers to life's greatest questions. Granted, we all need external support in order to accomplish desired ends, but if we never discover our true genius within, our means of reaching a destination may be misguided at best. We will find that the results we seek fall short of personal and professional fulfillment.

The well of life within is to be drawn out, not poured in by our trusted confidants. We must realize that who we are and what we have already exists in us; God placed it there. Our circles of family, friends, colleagues, and mentors have the role of drawing out the well of purpose within you.

Take note of your circle of close friends, family, and acquaintances right now. How are you relating to them? How are they relating to you? Is the relationship balanced? Do you find yourself continuously feeling drained after being in their presence?

Life giving is supposed to be reciprocal. If people are relating to you based on what you can give to them, the impact of that relationship will eventually leave you with a deficit. Perhaps you've been there before. When you notice a pattern of feeling like you've been drained of your energy after being with that group of people, it is an indicator of a relationship imbalance. People who constantly see you as someone who can help them, promote them, speak for them, save them, and bless them without a mutual exchange, will leave you depleted. If you are perpetually with that crowd, your emotional, psychological, physical, and spiritual tank can become empty as a result.

An interesting note: we tend to give others permission – sometimes unknowingly – to make withdrawals from our wells of life at will. It is amazing how much credit we give to others for *making* us do something, feel bad, or act the way we act. We use them as a sort of justification for any type of undesirable behavior. In other words, we give too much credit to others as the cause for our actions. When this occurs, we are essentially giving others permission to make withdrawals from our wells without price and respect to who we are.

Perhaps it's time for you to develop new circles of friends that will energize you to tap your well within. Seek out those who will push you to dig deeper and overcome barriers to achieving your purpose. And of course, the greatest of relationships, the one that will encourage and inspire you to greater levels of action and meaning, is a relationship with Jesus Christ.

Reason # 4: Purpose Informs Our Path

Today, so many of us travel along life's journey following a "cookie cutter" pattern. We tend to exist on the premises of how things were done or modeled for us. Whether it is due to anxiety or lethargy, we tend to avoid charting new territory in life.

Purpose exposes distinct qualities that provide inspiration for our path of discovery. Having a sense of purpose will illuminate a pathway toward fulfillment. All we need to do is take the next step. There is nothing as meaningless as walking down a dark path without light and having no sense of direction. Giving thoughtful consideration to our reason for being on earth, and paying close attention to what makes us come alive, can both become a channel for insight on our path.

Have you thought about your purpose long enough? Have you asked intimate questions about yourself that led to a greater awareness and respect for the value you bring to the world? If not, stop right here and now. Know that who you are matters! You matter because there's no one who can duplicate you. Your distinctive characteristics and personal makeup is what our world needs. If you choose to function at maximum capacity, you can make a lasting difference.

The human body is a unique and complex system comprising of numerous body parts and functions. Though our body parts are different, one part does not make a whole. All of our body parts together make us complete and who we are. Humanity as a whole runs on a similar system.

Imagine if we could all come to a place of knowing our purpose and begin to function in alignment with the rest of the world, rather than contrary to it. Yes, I know this sounds like a utopia, but progress towards this level of living begins with the individual. In so doing, the world would be a much better place.

Illumination of our own path can become possible when we consistently take interest in discovering our purpose and live true to our design. Have you ever had a period in your life where it seemed you were going around in circles as if you were on a merry-go-round? Have you had those periods in which you were only getting the same results in your personal life, work life, marriage life, or family life? "Round and round she goes, where she stops, nobody knows."

Purpose enables and empowers us to break self-defeating cycles of traveling down the road to nowhere. Purpose gives light to our paths, resulting in a meaningful, fulfilling life.

Reason # 5: Purpose Interests Us to Take Action

I want to introduce you to a very simple acronym to provide a mental picture for problem-solving and conceptualizing ideas. My prayer is that this acronym will empower you to move forward toward the ultimate discovery of who you are and a lifestyle of pursuing your God-given purpose.

There are times in our lives when we encounter situations that leave us feeling stuck and unsure about how to move forward or what to do to break free. Maybe you are at a stalemate in your career and you have reached the ceiling of progress and promotion. Perhaps you have become bogged down in your marriage and have reached a point of frustration and hopelessness where nothing you try seems to work. Perchance you have tried repeatedly to reach your son or daughter with parental wisdom, yet they do not seem to grasp your help, and you are at a loss for what to do next. Possibly, you have started out this year with high hopes that it will be the best year ever, but as time passes the less hopeful you become about living a life that really matters. Perhaps you see all too clearly that things are not working out as you hoped. There are too many scenarios to list in this writing, but the bottom line is figuring out how to deal with the dilemmas of our lives by moving from a place of stagnation to one of positive movement towards our goals.

I believe we all need a dependable *C.A.R.* When we find ourselves stuck or lacking forward momentum, nothing is more beneficial than the need for the right *Clarity*, giving insight for the right *Action*, which will produce the right *Results* (C.A.R.). Any time there is lack of progress in our lives, any time we suffer from immobility, it is a good cue to pause and regain clarity about who we are, and then refocus our energy on the reality of our purpose.

This line of thinking can add value to almost any environment. The idea of regaining clarity when solutions to problems appear scarce is about getting back to the basics of life. It is important in the step of clarity to give ourselves permission to slow down and reconnect with our core values and prioritize our goals. Ask yourself questions such as, "What was the purpose of starting school anyway? What was the reason for getting married in the first place? What values do I have that have been overlooked and need to be re-inserted in my decision-making process? Is there anything that I can do now in light of where I am that will help move me towards my goal while remaining true to my core? If so, what is it?"

Perhaps you might not find the answers to all the questions at one time, but being aware of and asking these questions is, in itself, a step in the right direction. It was not until later in life that some of these matters made sense to me. That is the picture of clarity and purpose each of us needs to understand; the idea of living your purpose is not a terminal, one-time event. It is a process to be lived out. The way it works is similar to putting pieces of a puzzle together. And the end result is every bit as satisfying.

Throughout my adulthood, I have occasionally reflected on conversations I had with my high school football coach who tried to convince me that I was good enough to play football at the college level. My coach would tell me that I was good enough. Sometimes, after our games, as we walked back to the locker room, my coach would ask the referee to tell me I was good enough to play in college. The problem was, no matter what my coach said, or what others said about my ability to play college football, I did not believe it myself. I had no internal clarity that I could play football at the next level.

What I realized later in life is that others can believe in you and know things about you, but if you are not clear yourself and do not know and believe in who you are, living your purpose in life can be limited. From the perspective of having a dependable C.A.R., I believe we all need to become clear there is potential in us, often hidden, that needs to be discovered and lived out.

What are some comments you have heard from others about you that recognizes your strengths, natural ability, and knack for doing things? It is good sometimes to listen from without as well as within. Ultimately, we must get clarity within that who we are is good enough to grow, develop, and make a difference in our world, but oftentimes a boost from an outside source can bring the inspiration or confirmation that we need.

Regaining clarity may take some time to do, but it is worth the time and energy. Doing so will allow space for making decisions based on principles rather than your emotions. For example, you can begin a statement with: "My name is (*fill in the blank*) and I am passionate about (*see if you can name at least three core values that guides your life, i.e. excellence, integrity, humility, empowerment, justice, love, teamwork*)."

You get the picture. These important values are the standards you choose to live by. If you have never considered your core values before, now may be a good time to pause, consider, and embrace your own set of core values. Our core values will ultimately drive our decision-making and our destinations on the journey of life.

If you have reached a point of dissatisfaction, before making a decision based on how you feel, consider what your dominant values are, and prioritize them before moving on. Quitting a job because you feel sad that you did not get the promotion, or leaving a marriage because you feel unloved, are decisions based on feelings and not principles. It is important to explore your primary values for making decisions. This set of principles will enable you to endure and persevere through tough times.

Once you gain some clarity about what is really important to you, you can chart a pathway for making sound decisions. Actions we take based on clarity of purpose will start a process of getting the results we truly want in life. The right clarity plus the right action will yield the right results.

Who's driving your C.A.R.? What is the basis of your C.A.R.? Where is your C.A.R. going? How's your C.A.R.

working for you? Do you have C.A.R. insurance? When was your last C.A.R. tune-up?

Do you have a C.A.R.?

If so, crank it up and let's get moving!

Explore points of I.R.A. as you reflect on Chapter Two and use the space provided to write areas of:

Identification – Look at areas in your life where you *identify* a need for a change. Thinking? Behavior?

Resignation – *Resign* from activities that hinder you from living your purpose.

Application – Ideas that can be *applied* as you maximize your potential. Think *application*.

Chapter Three

Five Action Steps toward Purpose

Determine not to waste another day without intentionally connecting with your purpose. Realize that your search begins with an inward dive. While pursuing and knowing your purpose will require work, it is not impossible. Clearly, the benefits of living a life of purpose far outweigh any costs or sacrifices along the wa . It is a journey well worth the efforts.

As a model for understanding better, connecting succinctly with, and living your purpose, here are five **A.C.T.I.O.N.** steps to assist you along the way.

Acknowledgement

Acknowledge where you are with integrity and honesty. The first step on the journey towards realizing your purpose and living it out is coming to terms with the truth of *who* you are, and *where* you are. Everything about you – your current circumstances, highs and lows, ups and downs, hopes and dreams, mistakes or failures – need to be identified. This is not for the sake of remaining where you are, but gaining wisdom to propel you forward.

At this stage, we tend to ask many "why" questions about the condition we are in. It is very important to shift our thinking from "why" to "what have I learned" or "what am I learning in this process?" Focusing on lessons learned creates a platform for strategic thinking and envisioning a future void of repeating the actions that produced unwanted results.

Go ahead and make peace with your past, quickly. "Yes, I did this. Yes, I did that. No, that was not the best way to handle that situation. Here is what I have learned, and I look forward to doing things differently today and in the future."

Confession

Confess mediocre behavior and commit to change. Confess means to admit, acknowledge, own up to, or come clean with. It is very easy to blame others for the conditions we find ourselves in. Perhaps in some instances, we are convinced that we are right in doing so. However, are there times when we could have done some things differently? Are there instances in which we gave what amounted to mediocre effort?

Granted, it really takes a mature person to examine him or herself and come clean with mediocre behavior. It is not easy, but do what you must to admit your role in the results you have gotten up to this point in your life. Conceding to our own role in the process is a step we all need to take if we want to move on with a greater commitment for change than before.

The motivation for change is borne out of a deep sense and belief of knowing you are not maximizing your purpose in life; therefore, there has to be more to life than what you are living. Confessing our role in the results we are getting and committing to change can awaken within us the value and need to use our time for maximum benefit.

Tailoring

Tailor your time. Here's some good news: we don't *have* to, but we *get* to look at how we are currently using our time in the development of our purpose. It is vital not to waste our time, as time is one of the most precious commodities we possess. You may say that, because of work or other requirements in your life, your time has already been set for you. This may be true, but how much time do you have left over after you have fulfille these obligations? How much time is spent on passive activities like watching TV, playing video games, having conversations with others via phone or in person that are going nowhere, or browsing through social media?

If we are going to live out our God-given purpose, the value we place in the stock of our time must go up. Over the next week, take an inventory of time busters in your life to see if there is any room for better use of your time.

Why is tailoring our time so important? We have one life to live. It is interesting how we can get more of many things, but time is one thing we cannot get more of. If use of time is not high on your priority list, make a change today. Begin to hold time in high esteem, and alter your use of time if necessary. The new purposeful use of your time can be filled with honing your craft, and learning more about your passion(s) in life. If you are not sure what your passion is, you can devote time in finding this out.

Modify your time to maximize moments of growing in your understanding of and living your purpose.

Investment

Invest in accountability. We were not created on an island, and we were not designed to go it alone in life. Fulfilling our purpose is not a solo act. It requires quality relationships where we both give to and receive from others.

Investing in accountability takes courage. It is not always easy to capitalize on developing honest relationships with others. Nonetheless, it is important to communicate with trusted people in our lives who we respect enough to hold us accountable to our inner and outer life.

Do you have a person who can be straightforward with you about any area of your life and ask you any question to check in and see how you are doing? Is there someone you trust to confront you in secret places? Are you willing, when challenged, to make the necessary changes? Or are you in a place where no one can tell you anything and you are unwilling to listen to anyone?

Investing in accountability is not something to be taken lightly. It needs to be embraced with the understanding that fulfilling our purpose depends on relationships of accountability. Who in your life right now can hold you accountable? This person or these persons may be hard to find, but it is worth the effort and time to seek out such relationships. In pursuing purpose, having a non-judgmental support structure in our lives is an invaluable resource.

Overcoming

Overcome your obstacles – everyone has them. The question is, "What will you do with yours?" Remember, you have people in your life, internal strength, and other written resources to help you in overcoming your obstacles.

I am reminded of a quote, "Hurdles were made to overcome." Living your purpose will not be an easy task. In fact, you will often be faced with seemingly insurmountable obstacles that sometimes make you want to give up and settle for a mediocre existence. The problems we face from day to day and how we handle them will provide opportunities for our unique genius to be on display.

Determine that you are an overcomer!

Negotiation

Negotiate or re-negotiate your goals and choose to live a life with no regrets. Life is a fast-moving train and our past builds up quickly. Today must be lived with a loose grip on our past, and a posture of respect for moving forward on purpose.

Let "living life with no regrets" be a value to live moment by moment from this day forward. Right now, it is important to negotiate or re-negotiate a new direction that will allow you to focus on taking steps necessary to improve who you are and where you are going. Stop now, if you have to, and give yourself permission to dream again, build again, and see again that your life truly matters.

A last-liner, do what you have to do in order to live your purpose! The world is waiting for your E.P.I.C. response!

Explore points of I.R.A. as you reflect on Chapter Three and use the space provided to write areas of:

Identification – Look at areas in your life where you *iden-tify* a need for a change. Thinking? Behavior?

Resignation – *Resign* from activities that hinder you from living your purpose.

Application – Ideas that can be *applied* as you maximize your potential. Think *application*.

Bibliography

Buford, Bob. *Halftime: Changing Your Game Plan from Success to Significanc* . Grand Rapids, MI: Zondervan, 1994. Print.

Edberg, Henrik. *" Gandhi's Top 10 Fundamentals for Changing the World.* The Positivity Blog, n.d. Web. 06 Mar. 2015.

Edwards, David C. *Motivation & Emotion: Evolutionary, Physiological, Cognitive, and Social Influences.* Thousand Oaks, CA: Sage, 1999. Print.

Random House Webster's Dictionary. New York: Ballantine, 2001. Print.

About the Author

D r. Daren Waters, Sr. is a pastor, life coach, motivational speaker, military veteran, husband, and father whose specialty is helping people negotiate life's transitions, find their life's purpose, and maximize their potential. Dr. Waters has over 21 years of experience in the discipline of helping others and connecting people to their purpose. He is a Licensed Marriage and Family Therapist with earned graduate degrees in Marriage and Family Therapy and Pastoral Counseling. He works professionally with individuals, couples, and families. You may find more about his services at www.valdostacoaching.net. Email: daren@valdostacoaching.net.

About the Book

*E*mbracing Your Identity and Living Your Purpose is designed to enable the reader to address matters such as core identity, inner purpose, and deep meaning in life. It will prime the pump of purpose within you, encouraging you to pursue a life filled with an undeniable reality of significanc

Embracing Your Identity and Living Your Purpose brings attention to the overarching question of "Who Am I?"

Author and Pastor Dr. Daren Waters Sr. addresses issues such as intentionally pursuing purpose and maximizing potential. It welcomes the reader to think about and explore the questions of, "What would my life be like if I knew my true purpose? What would my days look like if I pursued my purpose with a passion? What would my world look like if I encouraged others to find and explore their unique, God-given purpose?"

Embrace Your Identity and Live Your Purpose Today!